Mike Burton

HAVE BALLS
WILL TRAVEL

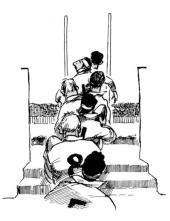

The Story of a Rugby Tour

Mike Burton

HAVE BALLS WILL TRAVEL

illustrations by Bill Tidy

Willow Books
Collins
St James's Place, London
1982

Willow Books
William Collins & Co Ltd
London · Glasgow · Sydney · Auckland
Toronto · Johannesburg

Burton, Mike
 Have Balls—will travel.
  1. Rugby football—Anecdotes, facetiae, satire, etc.
1. Title
 796.33'3'0207   GV945.2

First published 1982

ISBN 0 00 218005 7

Made by Lennard Books
The Old School
Wheathampstead, Herts AL4 8AN

Editor Michael Leitch
Designed by David Pocknell's Company Ltd
Production Reynolds Clark Associates Ltd
Printed and bound in Spain by
TONSA, San Sebastian
Dep. Legal SS 438/1982

CONTENTS

PREFACE

The rugby tour is the highlight of every season. I can well remember my first tour. A bus trip to London, before motorways were heard of, it entailed a steep climb out of my home city, Gloucester, then we went over the Cotswolds, past Oxford and on towards the capital. The present generation of young men would laugh at the idea of going to London on a tour, for they live in the age of the international tour. Nowadays, most clubs and schools embark at some time on an overseas tour and anything involving just a simple bus trip would be classed as an away game. Still, that first trip will live in my memory for ever.

We left on Friday night, watched England vs France at Twickenham on the Saturday afternoon and played a match against a local London team on the Sunday morning. I had been saving £1 a week since the beginning of the season and the treasurer told me as I boarded the bus that there was extra in the kitty because two lads had dropped out. That meant we could use their money for the beer, so my £4 10s spending money would go further than I had anticipated. It was my first mistake. By the time we had reached Northleach, a small village halfway between Gloucester and Oxford, my cash was running low and Richings, a flanker of doubtful reputation, was calling out from the front of the bus: 'OK, lads, £2 each will get a dozen more crates from this pub here.'

Richings turned out to be the star of the tour. After we had watched England stutter to a 3-point victory, we went out on the town. By midnight we had bumped into enough drunken Frenchmen to know that shouting 'Vive la France' went down well with our Continental visitors.

One of them was so pleased that he took off his newly purchased English bowler, and gave a low majestic bow. As the hand that held the bowler swept across the Frenchman's chest, Richings moved towards him. Quite unable to control the deep and sudden rumble he felt within himself, he had little option but to disgorge into the Frenchman's hat. The rest of us were off our blocks and running as Richings urgently called a halt. 'Hang on lads!' Back he went to the outraged visitor, stuck his hand in the hat and pulled out his false teeth.

I saw those teeth again the next day as our team deposited their watches, empty wallets and other personal treasure into the valuables bag before the match. Although the idea of playing a match on the way home seemed a good one when they'd asked us the previous September, now in the cold light of a January morning after two consecutive nights on the town, our enthusiasm had definitely faded. Still, play we did and despite the inevitable pasting we enjoyed the hospitality offered by our hosts afterwards as the story of Richings and the Frenchman's Hat rebounded round the clubhouse. I can't say that all the tours I went on were as coarse as that first outing, but rugby men are much the same the world over.

In this book I examine in detail the progress of an overseas tour, from the selection of the players to the problems of the touring pressmen and the pitfalls for a particular travel agent and his clients, the brave supporters who have quit their homes and loved-ones in the cause of international rugby.

GETTING THERE

The make-up of any touring team is essential. No matter how many good singers and personalities it contains the team will be judged solely by its performance on the field of play. As, this year, there is no Lions' Tour and none of the four home countries is committed to going overseas, a well-known rugby personality, Air Vice-Marshal Ken Quivermore, has asked  permission to take 20 players, a manager and a coach on a three-week venture abroad. The players are to be selected from England, Ireland, Scotland and Wales.

 A high-ranking Rugby Union official, Sir John Vaux-Tankard, grants permission subject to RFU Committee approval and provided he is manager and that the coach is a former Harlequin who has been to Cambridge. Quivermore agrees but insists that the team must bear his name, ie Air Vice-Marshal Ken Quivermore's XV, and that the coach must also have served at least three years as a commissioned officer in the RAF. After four days' deliberation Quivermore and Vaux-Tankard agree to appoint a part-time physical training instructor, Able Seaman Ivor Checks, as coach on the grounds that he was born in Cambridge, has a military background and saw the Harlequins lose a televised tug-of-war competition thirteen years ago. A further point in his favour is that  Checks knows nothing about rugby so will present no problems in selection meetings before or during the tour.

Quivermore and Vaux-Tankard have now to persuade the RFU Committee that a low-key, unofficial flag-waving tour is an acceptable alternative to a full-scale, heavy-artillery bloodbath with serious training and no drinking. A full meeting is convened to discuss selection policy (will we just choose nice chaps or will we actually have to watch them play before deciding who to take?) and the country or countries that are to be toured. Quivermore, Vaux-Tankard and Checks sit, rather like conspirators in the dock, on the opposite side of the room to the Committee of some fifty men gathered in strength and seated in banks of ten on five long tables which are draped in the green felt cloth normally seen on snooker tables. It promises to be the clash of the season, not excluding all the home internationals played this year plus the English and Welsh Cup Finals. The President himself opens the proceedings from the front table.

'Well, John. You already know that we as a Committee are opposed to any tour leaving these islands this year. . . .'

Before he can go any further Vaux-Tankard decides to interject. He speaks in a soft, almost nonchalant manner, hoping no-one will notice how hard he finds it to restrain himself.

'I fully appreciate the view of your Committee, Mr President. You have set aside this summer as a year when our best players can rest for next summer's Lions' Tour.'

The President nods, baffled by the cunning of this opening gambit, and Vaux-Tankard continues:

'But let me assure you that we wish to take 20 players, a coach, myself and Ken on a very low-key ambassadorial-type tour, preferably to a country that would benefit in rugby terms from our presence.'

Vaux-Tankard's face breaks into a smile as several Committee members sit back, fold their arms, and show mild interest in what he has to say. He grows expansive:

'You know, the hands across the sea. Meet the people. Spread the good name of Rugby Union, that sort of thing.'

Someone chips in from behind the President: 'That's all very well, but who's going to pay for this jaunt?'

Quivermore, until now calm and collected, shuffles the papers on the table in front of him without referring to them.

'Little jaunt,' he says, military severity creeping into his voice, 'I'll have you know that John, myself, Able Seaman Checks and the selected players will be giving up our annual holidays to accept the responsibility of this tour.'

A voice from the far corner of the room brings shouts of 'Hear, hear!' and 'Quite right!' when it says: 'Yes. But they're your bloody holidays, and what's more you want us to pay for them!'

'That is not what I'm suggesting.' Quivermore's face has reddened and he has unconsciously banged his clenched fist on the table. 'I think that some contribution should be made by the RFU or the Four Home Unions' Committee but the rest of the cost could be met by the money from the games we play on the tour.'

This meets with the approval of the Committee and it is suggested by one of the senior vice-presidents that 'We retire to the bar now we've got the meeting out of the way.'

'Just a minute.' Vaux-Tankard gets to his feet. 'Exactly how much do the Committee intend to contribute?'

The Committee members are a little annoyed that having achieved, as they thought, a brisk conclusion to the meeting and started towards the bar, they now have to find their places and sit down again. One North Country representative has lost his hearing aid and is on his hands and knees looking for it. The Chairman of the International Referee Selection panel, and a former referee himself, steps on his hand.

'Ouch! You bloody clown.'

'Sorry, sorry. I couldn't help it. I lost my specs on the train this morning.'

The apologetic referee feels his way along the chairs, comes to an empty one and plonks himself down.

The President is seething at his lack of ability to control the meeting. 'I never declared the meeting formally closed and furthermore I would remind you that this is not a piss-up.'

Just then six Committee men who had made it to the bar walk back in with trays of beers and spirits. The President does not notice them distributing the beverages along the various tables behind him as he gets the meeting underway again.

'A lot depends on which country you visit, John!' The President looks directly at Vaux-Tankard on the opposite table. 'I mean, South Africa, New Zealand. You would have enough gate money from say five matches there to pay for the return flight and three weeks' hotel accommodation.'

Quivermore nudges Vaux-Tankard with an elbow and whispers: 'We don't want either of those two countries. We'll be killed by their provincial sides and they'll try and con us into playing a Test or two.'

Vaux-Tankard doesn't need telling twice.

'Mr President,' he replies, 'I know that from a financial viewpoint both of these countries would be eminently suitable, but as I already said we ought to be taking the game of Rugby Union to a country that would benefit from our presence even if it does cost more money.'

Unbeknown to the President and senior vice-presidents on the front table, the members on the table behind them are getting quietly pissed and have sent one of their number out to organize fresh supplies of alcohol. Several of them have had enough to loosen their tongues.

'What about Australia or Fiji? They get big crowds.'

The President is not amused at what appears to be an unconstitutional comment by one of his Committee from the floor of the hall. Vaux-Tankard, after further prompting from Quivermore, takes up the point with some conviction:

'They're no different from South Africa or New Zealand. In those countries we would be presented with a hard physical confrontation and an atmosphere similar to that of a major tour and not at all conducive to flag-waving and hand-shaking.'

Checks settles back in his chair, his left leg crossed over his right and a 'that told 'em' look on his face.

The President resumes. 'What country would you recommend or prefer, John?'

'I think the Far East and/or Asia. Mr President, these countries rarely have a top-class touring team and I think our visit would do Rugby Union generally a lot of good.'

The President says: 'Yes, good point, John.'

Checks is beside himself with joy. He has been to those parts in his capacity as an able seaman and knows full well that the drink is cheap, women are even cheaper, and although as a race they try hard at rugby none of them can play. Moreover, their biggest men are around five feet eleven inches in their shoes.

Then a voice says: 'You might as well tour Jersey, Guernsey and the Isle of Man. They have not had an international team for over a century.'

The beer has really got to the members on the back table who are fed up with fetching trays all the time and have stacked up several crates of light ale at the end of the table and are passing them along, chain-gang style.

'Order! Order!' Even the senior vice-presidents have woken up to the din coming from the back of the room. The representative from the North, who has found his hearing aid, gets to his feet and gravely suggests that the tour should consist of five matches taking in Wigan, Oldham and Blackpool. He goes further, assuring Vaux-Tankard and Quivermore that they would be well looked after by the locals and, since the tour would not entail any air travel at all, it would be far cheaper.

The one bad thing, from where Quivermore, Vaux-Tankard and Checks are sitting is that no one laughs. Checks is mumbling under his breath: 'Please God they don't send us there. I left my first wife in Wigan, that's the last place I want to go.'

The President looks at his watch and licks his lips. The representative from Durham arrives from the table behind him with an armful of bottled ale. The President, visibly wilting under the pressure of temptation, smiles as if to reassure anyone in doubt that his dignity is not in question, then takes a long guzzle straight from the bottle. As soon as the taste gets to him, he calls a recess for lunch.

'But it's only 11.45,' says a voice on his left.

'Then we'll have a few jars before lunch, shall we?' says the President, a mock smile etched on his face.

In the bar next to the dining-room the real meeting gets under way. Vaux-Tankard, Checks and Quivermore are up and down the bar like clockwork mice, plying the President and his underlings with as much ale as they can deal with. The after-lunch session is short and to the point. Europe is swiftly knocked out on the grounds that it contains France, which ranks as unsuitable opposition. Then the President actually suggests a tour of the United States, playing five games, two in the East, one in the Midwest, one in Texas and one on the West Coast. The evidence of back-room dealing during the lunch hour is too much for the representatives from Sussex.

'They can't play rugby over there and three weeks in the hands of American women will affect our rugby players for the rest of their lives.'

Checks cannot restrain himself. 'What about the manager and coach? Do you think we'll get the chance to be affected as well?'

The meeting goes quiet as the Treasurer stands with a sombre expression on his face. 'One problem is of course that the gate money taken on games in the USA will not cover the cost of flights and hotel accommodation for 23 people.'

The President, only three parts pissed and dying to get back into the bar, gives a pledge. 'We'll pay for the return and internal flights and I'll arrange for our lads to be hosted by the families of the teams that they play against. This way we'll really make lasting friendships and rugby football will be the winner.'

Every single person in the room starts clapping and whistling. Quivermore, Vaux-Tankard and Checks shake hands vigorously and they walk across the divide between their table and the President's table to shake hands with the President. The President calls 'Order' once more and addresses the meeting on the point of selection:

'The team will be chosen by Air Vice-Marshal Ken Quivermore, Sir John Vaux-Tankard and the coach Able Seaman Ivor Checks. The team will be known as Air Vice-Marshal Ken Quivermore's XV and, as they are going to knock up a team during the next hour before they join us in the bar for the evening session, I declare the meeting formally closed.'

Within seconds the room is empty and Quivermore, Vaux-Tankard and Checks sit down to decide their travelling companions. It takes them 17 minutes to produce a team, 13 more to contact all of them by phone, another 10 minutes to rough out profiles on the players, and one minute to get back in the bar.

The team sheet, with profiles, was short and to the point. When John Fairchild, the *Sunday Cable's* controversial rugby correspondent, found out who was going, he wrote his own set of character-studies, which appeared as follows:

FULL-BACK

Dai Usher
5ft 11in 14st 6lb
Wales and British Lions
This fearless young medical student has won a place in the hearts of rugby fans everywhere and scored more tries than anyone in last year's Five Nations' Championship. Not considered arrogant but surprised everyone this season when seen talking to a hooker during a break in play; successfully sued a TV commentator for saying he missed a tackle. Has been offered big money to write an autobiography but says he wants to stay in the game.

17

WING

K K Courage
5ft 5in 11st 0lb
Wales and British Lions
Fastest man in the team. Would be a
worldbeater if he could tackle. Seen at his best
when standing at the bar waiting for something
to happen or chipping pint glasses over the
barmaid's head. Sales representative.

WING

J V Charrington
5ft 2in 8st 12lb
Oxford University and England
The slowest of the backs on tour but makes up
for lack of speed by being the most persuasive
conversationalist. His mother was very close to
Air Vice-Marshal Quivermore as a schoolgirl.
Assistant mill manager.

CENTRE

Les Ansell
6ft 14st 3lb
England
This likeable young centre, just recovered from a badly broken arm, is sure to be a popular tourist. He will tackle anything. Once met a police car going the wrong way round a roundabout and came off best. Described by the senior members of his club side as a playful puppydog. Recently began work as a trainee corset-maker.

CENTRE

Sean O'Guinness
5ft 11in 13st 6lb
Ireland and British Lions
This Irish flyer will be a steady influence on the team. A devout non-smoking, teetotal Roman Catholic. Thinks contraceptives are luxury balloons for wealthy children. Should add flair and class to the backs. Apprentice priest.

UTILITY BACK

Willie Younger
5ft 10½in 13st 8lb
Scotland and British Lions
An incisive runner from the full-back position with experience on the wing, in the centre and at outside-half. Ace goal-kicker, favours tight-fitting, extremely short shorts, has a beautiful smile and can't tackle to save his life. Hairdresser.

OUTSIDE-HALF

Julian Tetley-Simpkiss
5ft 7in 10st 10lb
Uncapped
Just out of school and yet to find a club to join. He is the twin brother of the prop Jeremy and nephew of Air Vice-Marshal Quivermore. Looks and talks like a real prick but sure to get plenty of games with his uncle picking the team. Recently applied for a job as a dressmaker.

SCRUM-HALF

Keith Watney
5ft 6in 10st 3lb
England
The most popular selection of the whole party. Can spin-pass further off his left hand than his right. Has an infectious grin, is sure to develop as the team's leading comedian. Recently came off a diet that lost him three stones. Is currently impressing six local maidens at once with his new-found stamina and zest for life. Fishmonger.

SCRUM-HALF

Rodney Eldridge-Pope
5ft 2in 8st 6lb
England
Lucky to get time off from his job as a children's programme presenter with London Weekend Television, but looks like making a full contribution to the tour as a world-class line-out signal reader.

PROP

Nogger Bass
6ft 2in 18st 5lb
St Luke's College
This thoroughly clean-living young man impressed all the other students when arriving for his first training session with his short back and sides and his bright white Woolies' pumps. Is reputed to be able to sleep anywhere at any time and is the man most forwards prefer to stand behind if the other team cuts up rough.

PROP

Hamish 'Topcat' Haig
5ft 10in 16st 7lb
Scotland and British Lions
Known among the front-row union as a pocket battleship with more than one gun. Knows all the songs and is certain to be choirmaster. On previous tours his reputation for being as tight as a pig's ear has ensured him the job of kittyholder as well. Lecturer on sexual techniques.

PROP

Jeremy Tetley-Simpkiss
5ft 7in 10st 10lb
Uncapped
Shocked everyone by turning up at a recent home game with his uncle, the manager, wearing a double-breasted blazer and a cravat. Has no experience of propping except from his schooldays. The rest of the team are rumoured to have requested that the two Tetley-Simpkisses are never allowed to play in the same game on tour as they cannot carry two wankers at once. Unemployed.

HOOKER

Ben Bulmer
5ft 9in 12st 2lb
England and British Lions
The burly Bulmer promises to challenge Watney as the team comedian and is certain to lead in the beer-drinking stakes. A conscientious trainer with a permanently podgy appearance, he hides his embarrassment about being overweight with an outrageous personality and his shirt when having sex. Yes! Refuses to take his shirt off whilst at it, in case his wife, or mistress, sees his paunch. Trainee airline pilot.

HOOKER

Jim 'Piston' Skolar
5ft 10in 14st 3lb
Wales and British Lions
Not the fastest of strikers but hasn't lost one against the head since he killed the opposing hooker in the second scrum of a cup match two years ago. Should be first choice for hooker on tour if his hamstring holds up.

LOCK (CAPTAIN)

Stan Mackeson
6ft 3in 16st 7lb
England and British Lions
This amiable son of a Yorkshire mill owner has been the backbone of England's effort in recent years with his single-minded determination to succeed. Has vowed to win all the games on tour and will stand no pissing about from the ranks. Sales manager.

LOCK

Archie McEwan
6ft 4in 16st 3lb
Scotland and British Lions
A hard drinker and a hard player. Should prove a valuable tourist. Has been to all parts of the rugby-playing world and is prepared to die in his boots rather than lose a game.

LOCK

J M Ruddle
6ft 6in 17st 8lb
England and British Lions
The backbone of the touring team's line-out. Considered posh by his team mates with his slow City of London accent. Hates training, is a consistent chain-smoker and lives for the final whistle. Insurance agent.

OPEN-SIDE FLANKER

Tony Everard
5ft 8in 14st 2lb
England
Has everything a man wants. Tall, pacy, handsome, qualified accountant, international rugby star. His personal dimensions are the envy of his team-mates. This smooth-talking flyer spends his time fighting off amorous females. Became very popular when he started passing them on to his less fortunate colleagues. Should make a full contribution on the field of play as well.

NO 8

Alan Theakston
6ft 6in 15st 5lb
England
An all-round athlete. Could have been an Olympic runner if he had stayed off the marijuana but still a superb player and one all the other members of the team measure themselves against in training.

BLIND-SIDE FLANKER

Tom Carling
5ft 11in 17st 1lb
Ireland trialist
Local lager-drinking champion. Works as a steamroller driver during the day and trains on weights most nights. This former heavyweight boxing champion looks like being a great tourist but is frightened of flying and has applied unsuccessfully to leave a week early by boat.

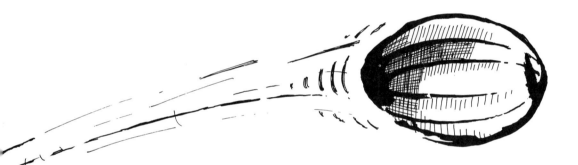

THE FLIGHT

After arriving in London for the issuing of tour kit—blazers, flannels, tie, boots, etc—the boys head off to Heathrow and the flight out. Watney is already into the tour as fever begins to grip the unfortunate Carling.

'Hey, Tom, get a few brandies down you before take-off. You'll be OK.' Watney grins from ear to ear and adjusts his new tour tie in the coach-driver's rearview mirror. Dai Usher offers some kind of anti-fear pill. Ruddle leans forward from behind yesterday's *Times*, a freshly lit cigarette in his hand.

'Is there any possibility of our pack being issued with those before each match?' he asks the young medic.

Nogger sneers as he nudges Piston: 'Typical London ponce!'

'Aye, we always give them some of that when they come down the valleys,' says Skolar, pointing to his polished Chelsea boot.

Checks is already trying hard to establish some sort of authority by staying sober and marching up and down the coach gangway and stopping every few minutes for impromptu chats with various members of the squad. Quivermore and Vaux-Tankard are laughing away in the front seat of the coach as they see off the contents of a silver hipflask.

The airport lounge resembles Grimsby fishmarket on a Monday morning. Bodies are flying in every direction. The team are easily recognized by their smart blazers, shirts and tour ties, which is more than can be said for the 39 supporters booked to follow the tour. They are wandering all over the terminal like sheep without a dog to keep them in order. The Pressgang of nine Fleet Street scribes are fuming as they will not be on the same flight as the team and have been demoted to the level of tour supporters. Even worse news is to come. The airline carrying the supporters and press has been on strike for a week. It looks like a three-day delay which means they will miss the first match. Everyone is up in arms against the travel agent, Jim Messingham, who should have known better.

The team are glad to get on board their own flight, change to tracksuit bottoms and T-shirts and settle back with earphones plugged in whilst the press and supporters face up to a long wait. Even at this early stage the tour comedians begin to emerge. Watney and Bulmer have chosen plum aisle seats so they can run their hands up the hostesses' legs as they serve the in-flight goodies. Bass and Ruddle are well on the way to being pissed. Everard has already pulled the four hostesses on board who are fighting for the right to serve him, while McEwan and Mackeson dutifully discuss the tactical approach to the tour.

This is just as well because Quivermore, Vaux-Tankard and Checks are sleeping off the effects of free in-flight drinks and look like missing the first selection meeting, scheduled to take place in the area between the aft toilets after dinner. McEwan suggests to Mackeson that they co-opt two new members onto the selection committee to replace Quivermore and Checks ('just for the first meeting'). The new men should be three-quarters so that someone on selection knows something about what happens outside the scrum. K K is summoned from the bulkhead bar and Dai Usher is woken from a self-induced sleep to contribute to the selection of the team.

'Right, full-back first,' says the skipper.

'Right, I'll do that.' Usher is already writing his name against the number 15.

'OK. Left-winger.'

K K writes in his own name without a word being said.

'Centres?'

At that moment the toilet door bangs shut as Ansell disappears with a young lady he has been talking to since take-off. Mackeson chimes in:

'Ansell and O'Guinness. Give Younger a run-in at outside-half.'

Everyone nods.

'Right wing?'

'J V Charrington?'

'Christ! Do we have to play him so early in the tour?'

Mackeson nods thoughtfully. 'If we give him a run-out early it will please Vaux-Tankard and Quivermore to have an Oxford Blue in the team, and there's a good chance he will get injured before the hard games come along.'

'Bloody good thinking,' grins K K. 'Give Tetley-Simpkiss a game at prop, put Eldridge-Pope at scrum-half and that's the Establishment happy.'

Dai Usher, brought in to selection for his knowledge of three-quarter play, now throws his effort into front-row selection. 'If Tetley-Simpkiss plays, put Nogger and Piston in or he'll get bloody killed. We can always put Topcat in with Nogger later in the tour.'

'OK. Sounds good.'

Stan's pen scratches its way down the team sheet.

'OK. Locks?'

Mackeson looks at McEwan and begins to write in both their own names.

'But you're both front jumpers.'

Both locks fix their eyes on the dissenting Usher.

'Sorree.' Usher's eyes begin to scan the aircraft floor.

'Back row?'

Just then the bog door opens and out comes the perspiring Ansell, hand-in-hand with his new-found friend. Stan tries hard to ignore it and pretends to be writing. But Ansell refuses to be quiet and is shouting something about club membership and being over a mile in the air. This is enough to wake both Quivermore and Vaux-Tankard who spring to their feet, and while Quivermore issues a bollocking to Ansell, Vaux-Tankard suggests to Stan that they have a selection meeting. After explaining that the team was all but selected, and that only one of the Tetley-Simpkiss twins was in the team, Stan puts his pen away and disappears into the toilet. Meanwhile Vaux-Tankard has told the coach, Checks, what a failure he is for sleeping instead of being at the selection meeting and nods agreement with Quivermore's assertion that the back row should be Everard, Theakston and the other Tetley-Simpkiss.

'But he's an outside half!'

'Shut up. I told their mother that they would have at least one game together on the tour.'

Quivermore is furious that anyone should argue with his decision. The bog door opens and Stan whistles his way back into the meeting.

'Tetley-Simpkiss in the back row! Have you all gone stark staring mad?'

No-one makes a move. Quivermore points a finger.

'Look, Stan, he's a perfectly worthwhile chap and he will do a jolly good job for us even if he is out of position.'

Mackeson shrugs and shoves the team sheet into Quivermore's hand, then stumbles up the gangway for a drink.

NEW YORK, NEW YORK

On arrival at JFK Airport each of the lads is handed an itinerary. It reads:

Saturday May 10 Arrive JFK Airport. Met by sister of the President of NY Prison Warders' XV. (*Note* Have only just been informed that you are coming by the President of the RFU so we have not had time to fix up hosting. You are all in a motel until after the first match on Wednesday.)

Travel by service bus to the SKYLARK HOTEL, 144 54 5th Street, Manhatten. Meet the President of New York Prison Warders' XV who will be in the downstairs bar. Check in for four nights on bed-and-no-breakfast basis and pay your own account.

Sunday May 11 6.30am Training. 1pm Visit the prison, watch concert specially staged by the inmates. 11.30pm Return to Hotel. (*Note* This concert is particularly long and has to be staged in four quarters. Cups of tea will be available in each interval.)

Monday May 12 6.30am Training. 11.30am Take part in sponsored run (18 miles) on behalf of fund for the deprived children of the inmates. 4pm Free use of gymnasium, swimming pool and basketball facilities. (*Note* As the jail is maximum security you cannot be released until the 11.30 warden shift changes, then you may leave with the staff and retire to your hotel.)

Tuesday May 13 6.30am Training. 1pm Walk up Empire State Building. See New York as you have never seen it before. 5pm Brewery visit. Free beer will be served from 5pm until 3am.

Wednesday May 14 Match Day. 2.30pm Kick off versus New York Prison Warders' XV, venue New York State Penitentiary Games Field. Passes to get in will be issued to those travelling on the team bus only. After-match reception at the British Embassy.

Thursday May 15 9.30am Depart New York for Boston by coach. Afternoon Met by families for hosting.

Friday May 16 Meet for training on the field behind the brewery where you will be spending the afternoon and evening.

Saturday May 17 Match Day vs Boston All Stars. (*Note* If unable to find the venue of the match ring Ed Schultz on 617/399/4441.) Evening reception at The Old Bull and Bear (English beer served).

Sunday May 18 am Training, then depart Boston to Chicago by coach.

Monday May 19 Arrive Chicago. Rest all day. Play most of the night.

Tuesday May 20 am Training. pm Visit brewery. (*Note* Sampling available.)

Wednesday May 21 Match Day vs Chicago Maulers. 5.30pm Free medical treatment is available from Dr Rick Dabonski (Maulers' member for 12 years) who appreciates National Health treatment he received at Wapping General Hospital during the 1981 Maulers' UK tour.

Thursday May 22 Depart from O'Hare International Airport for Texas. Met on arrival by host families of Texas Tigers RFC.

Friday May 23 am Training. pm Visit the biggest pie-making plant in Texas. (Free samples available on departure but not for resale.) Evening visit Texas Brewery for beer and pie party.

Saturday May 24 Match Day vs Texas Tigers.

Sunday May 25 Party departs for Los Angeles. Met by hosts from Los Angeles Ladies' College of Art and Drama where dormitory accommodation has been provided.

Monday May 26 Recover from the first night's rest.

Tuesday May 27 am Training. pm Visit wineries. Free wine-tasting throughout the afternoon. Transport to and from the vineyards supplied by Ladies' College own bus. Any problems (ie lost, drunk, skint) contact Suzie Schulman at the Hall of Residence on 213/603/1179.
Wednesday May 28 Match Day vs Los Angeles Rams. After-match reception at the College.
Thursday May 29 The tour is at leisure from today, although you will remain in residence at the college until your flight home on Sunday.
Friday May 30 At leisure.
Saturday May 31 At leisure.
Sunday June 1 Depart Los Angeles International Airport for London.

The boys are astounded. No hosting! President's sister to meet us, training at 6.30 in the morning! The first part of the tour looks more like a bloody commandos' training course! Up at 6.30, sponsored run, concert organized by prisoners. Quivermore is even more astonished. He turns to Vaux-Tankard:

'Do you realize they have got a brewery or vineyard visit the night before every game? We will never control them.'

Vaux-Tankard barks: 'Don't worry. They're never going to fool us like that.'

On the bus from the airport the sister of the President, who is escorting the team to the Skylark Hotel, is sitting on Checks's knee with her hand inside his shirt and telling him how she always wanted an Englishman, also her husband works nights most weeks. There is a yell from the back of the bus. Nogger Bass has just seen the final part of the itinerary and he rushes to the front of the bus waving the partly-torn sheet under the nose of the lady on Checks's knee.

He asks: 'This college we are at for five days. Is it all ladies there?'

'Oh! my son. There are three thousand girls there all in residence.'

As one, the rest of the bus turn the pages of their itineraries. Skolar cannot believe it. 'Christ! Three thousand birds and only twenty-three of us!'

38

'Twenty-two!' cries O'Guinness. 'I do not wish to be involved in that sort of thing.'

'Please your bloody self.'

Carling looks across the aisle at O'Guinness and then turns to look out of the window, his mind riveted on Los Angeles and the last five days of the tour.

The bus pulls to a halt outside the hotel. After checking in, the team go off to bed in ones and twos while the management go into the night to negotiate with the President of the New York Prison Warders' Club about reducing the scheduled number of functions and brewery visits.

TRAINING

The first morning in New York is full of excitement and expectation. The tracksuited figure of Ivor Checks walks out to the centre of the training field, whistle around his neck, and watches the boys warm up. They have half a dozen balls between them. The props and locks play at drop goals and the balls screw off towards the corner-flags. The three-quarters jog up and down in pairs, chatting and flicking the ball casually between them.

'OK, lads! Come in please. Form a circle. I'm going to give you the team for the tour-opener. Let me say first of all that we can only choose fifteen at a time so some of you will be disappointed. Those not selected this time will play on Saturday.'

The boys listen intently to the announcement that both Tetley-Simpkisses will play, with one in the back row, and then on Checks's instructions begin lapping the field, slowly at first but then speeding up to a pace fast enough to separate the backs from the forwards.

'OK! Run on down to the try-line, please, lads. Take some deep breaths, that's right, get it into you before we start the circuit.'

It's a chance for the lads to consult. Topcat is first with his assessment. In a rasping Scottish accent he says: 'Did you hear that? You might as well play my wife in the back row as play him.'

Nogger shows open contempt as Checks barks his orders:

'OK, find yourself a partner. Backs with backs. Forwards with forwards.'

Bass grabs Tetley-Simpkiss.

'I say, I think I'll find a three-quarter partner.'

'No you bloody well won't.' Nogger holds him firmly by the shirt front. 'You'll stay with me.'

'Wheelbarrow position, please.' The coach is determined to make the training interesting and competitive.

Bass offers no choice of who will do the wheelbarrowing and who the pushing. He leers across to his team-mates as he holds the unfortunate Tetley-Simpkiss by the ankles. Before Checks can start them off, and while all the others are lining up along the goal-line for the trip upfield, Bass pushes the outside-half-cum-flanker as if to ram his head into the centre of the earth.

'Come on, you little runt. You'll have to get used to this in the back row, won't you?'

Every member of the team is falling about with laughter, except Tetley-Simpkiss's twin brother and Quivermore.

'Careful now, Nogger. He's only a young lad, you know.'

Quivermore decides to bring his nephew off the field. The session finishes with a series of sprints and a three-mile run back to the team's hotel where for the first time the lads share a shower and a cold beer. The sight of Everard and O'Guinness in the altogether proves too much for some. Tom Carling, who missed the training session because he was still recovering from airsickness, and is still not wholly recovered, catches sight of both men advancing towards him. He falls unconscious to the floor. Five minutes later he is sitting propped up on a bench explaining that he thought he was being attacked by a brace of white elephants.

Vaux-Tankard, Quivermore and Checks enter for an informal chat, ie a friendly warning that the first game is two days away and that due caution should be applied in off-duty time and normal standards of

discipline applied during training sessions. Nineteen pairs of eyes glaze over.

TABLE TALK

The team amble towards the dining-room in small groups and pairs, chatting about the weather and what they have just seen hanging freely from below the waists of Everard and O'Guinness. Skolar can't get his mind off the subject.

'Do you reckon O'Guinness ever has any practice with it? He lives in a monastery now, you know, and he's dead serious about taking vows and all that.'

Ruddle, walking slightly in front of Skolar, stops and turns:

'Of course he's had practice with it. How do you think it got that big?'

Several steps further on, and after considerable thought, Skolar replies:

'Well, I've had stacks of practice and mine isn't that big.'

The boys are still laughing as they take their places at the long team table for the first meal together. O'Guinness and Everard are sitting opposite Ruddle, Nogger and Skolar, with Dai Usher between them. O'Guinness is the only one to say grace as Skolar cracks into a piping-hot curry. It is all too much for Tom Carling who leaves the table in a rush. Bulmer arrives late and tucks into Carling's half-finished salad before ordering a large steak and chips. Skolar is still shaking his head as he eyes O'Guinness and Everard, then he points his fork at Usher (the medical student) and asks:

'Tell me, Dai, do you think they get any bigger when they are erect or do they stay the same size and just go hard?'

O'Guinness is appalled by such conversation and says so.

'All right,' says Skolar. 'No need to get nasty, now. Anyway, if you were a real priest you wouldn't get all stroppy like that, would you!'

No reply. Skolar turns his attack on the cool Tony Everard who is politely refusing steamed pudding and asking for coffee.

'White with no sugar, please.'

'Well, do *you* reckon you are bigger than the rest of us when you are ready to perform?'

Tony sips his coffee thoughtfully. 'I don't know. I've never seen any of you when you are about to perform and what's more I have absolutely no intention of letting you see me in a similar position.'

Silence. Skolar orders his pudding. Ruddle lights his 39th cigarette of the day and puffs his considered opinion over Skolar's pudding and Nogger Bass's face:

'I really do think you have become obsessed with this subject, you know, Jim.'

Before Skolar can reply, Bass steams in, holding up a large clenched fist.

'Yes, and you'll be obsessed with this if you keep smoking and blowing it all over me.'

Ruddle, without reply, slowly rises from the table, knocks the ash from the end of his cigarette into his coffee saucer and saunters towards the dining-room door, inwardly desperate that no-one should think he was running away from Bass. The rest of the day is spent playing cards in the bedrooms. Mackeson and McEwan are a little concerned that high sums of money are being won and lost, but neither complains too loudly as the great god Team Spirit is unlikely to be affected.

FIRST MATCH

Soon it is Wednesday and time for the first match of the tour. No-one thinks of anything else from the moment he wakes up. Some lads have breakfast in bed. Some take nothing or just coffee. At eleven o'clock there is a team talk in Stan's room. Everyone is present except the Tetley-Simpkiss who has been selected to play on the flank.

'Where is the little runt?'

Stan is furious. He never wanted him in the team anyway, playing out of position and depriving a good player of a game, and now he's late for the team talk.

'Someone go to his room and get him.'

Bass rises quickly to his feet. 'No. Er, thank you, Nogger.' Stan is not slow to realize that Tetley-Simpkiss would be in no condition to play if Bass got his hands on him. 'You go, Bulmer.'

The bulky hooker is setting off for the missing man's room when there in the doorway, a cup of coffee in one hand and piece of toast in the other, dressed in silk pyjamas bearing his initials on the left breast, stands Tetley-Simpkiss.

'Terribly sorry to keep you waiting.'

Nobody says a word, although Bass is unable to prevent his upper lip from rolling up in one corner as he expresses his primitive contempt for the novice flanker. Then Stan launches into his talk:

'We have a job of work to do here today. Eighty minutes' hard work.' He slaps his clenched fist into his palm. 'It's no good approaching this like a charity match, these bloody warders have been handling murderers and villains every day for years.'

Dai Usher says his piece to the backs about alignment, tackling, speed of the ball through the hands and how they should attack from deep positions off bad kicks from their opponents. When the room empties, confidence is oozing from everyone in the team, except Bass who still has little faith in either Tetley-Simpkiss.

The coach trip to the prison is a quiet, almost sombre affair. No-one

feels much like talking. The adrenalin has been pumping almost since breakfast-time. None of the forwards has shaved except both Tetley-Simpkisses. At the ground they file into the dressing-room and look at the programme which has been printed in the prison workshop. Each player stuffs a few into his kit-bag for souvenirs, then they walk onto the field for the rituals of digging a heel into the top surface, throwing up blades of grass, and wetting a finger to see which side dries first, then back, silently and deliberately, to the dressing-room.

Each member of the team prepares in his own individual way. Ansell changes completely except for his boots, which are highly polished with new white laces and sit next to his kit-bag like two sentries at Buckingham Palace.

'I'll put them on at the very last minute,' he says to Stan who is going round talking to them all in turn. Some need cajoling, others need cooling, some need motivating. Coach Ivor Checks stands in the centre of the room.

'OK. Everyone sit down.'

Checks sounds off with an in-depth account of their weaknesses and our strengths. Confidence is high as the lads troop into the tunnel, the replacements tracksuited and carrying a variety of shin-pads and sticky tapes in their hands. Up into the daylight. As the noise of 5,000 criminals hits their ears, their thoughts run away with them. 'Christ! There must be 70,000 here.' A glance across at their team. The minds of our lads are momentarily blown. 'Christ, I've never seen a pack as big as that.' 'Hope we win the toss and kick off.' 'Look at that one sprinting!' 'Yes, and he's only warming up.'

The worst happens. Stan loses the toss and they kick off. 'Never mind,' think the forwards, 'we'll weather that first bang. Bind over the catcher, get the ball away and we're in the game.' The ball is falling through the air. A murderous pack is homing in on our lads.

'My ball!'

Binding in on that lone brave voice is the only thought in the mind of each forward. How could they have been so naive? It was that prick Tetley-Simpkiss, now realizing he will have to stay true to his word and catch the bloody thing. Naturally, he gives it straight to their bloke to save himself from unnecessary punishment. The 18-stoner has accepted his gift with glee and crashed into J V Charrington who has fallen over himself trying to get out of the way.

After one minute Air Vice-Marshal Ken Qivermore's XV are 4—0 down and Charrington is having to leave the field. This finds Checks in a difficult situation. Julian Tetley-Simpkiss, the outside-half, is already on the field as a back-row forward. Tom Carling has to go on to replace him, with Julian transferring to the wing to take the place of Charrington. Carling, of course, has not recovered from his upset stomach and has had the runs all morning. Off with the tracksuit and onto the field he goes, only to be told by Tetley-Simpkiss that he will have to play on the wing:

'There's no way I'm playing against that fifteen-stone even-timer they've got for a winger.'

Carling is too ill to argue and trots over to the wing position while Mackeson, McEwan and Bass threaten Tetley-Simpkiss with certain death if he stays in the pack. Tactics are always decided by a team's strengths and weaknesses, and with this in mind the opposing team start moving the ball to Carling's wing at every opportunity. The result is a glut of tries leaving the lads 16—0 down at half time; without the courageous tackling of Dai Usher it would have been a lot more.

The second half sees a change in the tourists' approach. Mackeson has decided that if they keep the ball within three yards of the decent forwards they have on the field, they might bring the opposition down to the level of the two Tetley-Simpkisses in their own pack and at the same time save Carling from the embarrassment of bouncing off his opposite number yet again. Mackeson has an even better idea as the last ten minutes approach:

'Each one of you in our pack take a turn at hitting either Tetley-Simpkiss when you're sure the ref will see him go over. I happen to know he's serving life for triple murder. He'll never believe his own team-mates would do such a thing, and give *us* the penalties.'

In five minutes Bass has hit both of them twice and the tourists are only 12–16 down. With Bass in this mood they may even sneak a win. But no need. After a brilliant move involving each of the backs except Carling, Usher goes over in the corner. 16–16 with the injury-time kick to come. Sean O'Guinness steps up for his big moment. Skolar frowns. How can he kick with an obstruction like that between his legs. Sean hits it high and clean and misses by inches. 'I told you din' I!' Skolar sprints off to the dressing-room as the whistle goes. An honourable draw.

THE SHOWER

Into the dressing-room they troop, where Checks is congratulating everyone on a great comeback. Quivermore is very concerned about his twin nephews. Both of them have black eyes and blood trickling from the mouth. J V Charrington is sitting in the corner, one arm in a sling. No-one pays him any attention. Skolar peels off his kit slowly, waiting for O'Guinness and Everard to cross the changing-room with their now-famous showpieces there for all to see. Just then, as if stage-managed, they stroll together towel in hand right past Skolar towards the steam of the shower-room. Skolar looks at Ansell.

'Christ! Britain would be the richest place on earth if we could grow more like that and export them!'

Quivermore is beaming as he pats his little pets and shakes the hand of Ivor Checks warmly. 'Well done, Ivor. You certainly got these boys in condition.' Then, flushed with excitement, he addresses the team from the top of a large wicker basket which carries the kit.

'Gentlemen. Tonight we face our first public engagement as a team. The post-match reception will be held at the British Embassy and we must give a good account of ourselves. You are ambassadors each and every one of you. I want you to be courteous to the thirty-two young ladies who will be present at the reception because they are the wives and daughters of the Embassy staff and officials. You will, of course, wear your full Number One tour outfit, blazers, white shirts, ties, flannels and black shoes. Thank you and have a lovely evening, but remember the bus leaves at 9.30 in the morning for Boston. Oh! And just so we don't appear rude, say goodbye to your opposite number before we leave this place because they will not be attending tonight's function.'

THE RECEPTION

The whole of Air Vice-Marshal Quivermore's planning goes up in smoke as the supporters and press party arrive just in time to gate-crash the reception. Pressmen are literally tearing around the reception to get a blow-by-blow account of what happened. Who scored? Who was injured? Anyone make a mistake? Quivermore and Vaux-Tankard call an impromptu press conference in the hallway.

'All I can tell you,' says Quivermore, his hands held up to stop the pushing and shoving, 'is that our three best players have all been pretty badly injured, but I think they will be OK for the next match.'

'Who? Who?' The pressmen push for details.

'J V Charrington and the Tetley-Simpkiss twins.'

Across the world the wires carrying the names of the three unlikely heroes could have snapped under the weight of conscience, for next morning the story would be there for all the world to read.

Meanwhile Skolar and Topcat have talked O'Guinness and Everard into entertaining four young ladies in the main bedroom of the house where there are grand chandeliers, a large piano and three four-poster beds. Bulmer, Theakston and Ruddle have asked respectfully if they can come along to watch. The ladies took no convincing at all and the only stipulation they made was that the bedroom door be locked.

O'Guinness, it must be said, does not quite understand his predicament as everyone except himself and the three spectators, Theakston, Bulmer and Ruddle, begins to undress. One glimpse of Everard naked convinces the four young ladies that he is for them.

50

Topcat and Piston stand, hands on hips, waiting to grab anyone Everard cannot manage.

Piston nudges Topcat: 'He's never going to manage four of them is he?'

O'Guinness is now making strenuous efforts to get out. Ruddle and Theakston are holding him back but Bulmer suggests they let him go as it would leave a spare woman for them to share between the three of them. O'Guinness continues the fight and in the struggle his pants end up around his ankles, placing the four young ladies in the difficult position of choosing between the Irish neophyte and Everard. O'Guinness looks the better bet, and he is already on the floor and being held by Ruddle. Eager female hands grasp *TINKLE* for their prize.

TINKLE

'Please, please!' begs Sean. 'Aaaah!'

Bulmer is laughing so much he spills his beer. Theakston and Ruddle rip off their clothing and, with Guinness's opposition ended, eleven nimble bodies jump into the biggest four-poster bed in the room.

TWO SHORT... SOMEONE'S IN THE CHANDELIERS!

51

ON THE ROAD

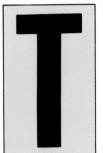

The long bus journey the next morning is not made any better for Bulmer by the discovery after the event that his partner in the night was the mother of the other three. O'Guinness is beside himself with disgust at being lured into such a trap. Watney and Ansell are sulking.

'You could have bloody well called us in at around three in the morning for a share of the action. Call yourself team-mates?

Mackeson and McEwan shield their eyes from the light and swear they will never drink spirits again. J V Charrington and the twins share the back seat. Vaux-Tankard and Quivermore are snoozing in the seat behind the driver. Watney has squeezed shaving foam all over their heads with a short note slipped into the top pocket of the manager saying it was Ivor Checks, who is sleeping on the other side of the aisle. Topcat has stolen a team-mate's camera and has taken a full frontal photo of K K posing with his pants down. As he calmly slips the camera back into the owner's kit-bag, Dai Usher cracks up at the thought of the camera-owner's wife taking the film into the chemist and innocently asking for enlargements.

The stop for lunch brings howls of protest from Vaux-Tankard and Quivermore.

'Who squeezed this stuff all over us?'

No-one answers, but no-one is laughing either. Possibly the dirtiest trick ever seen on a rugby tour anywhere in the world is about to be played. In the restaurant J V Charrington points accusingly with his one good arm at Watney. The pressmen are there, having caught up with the team bus. Instantly they drop knives, forks, bread rolls, serviettes, and surround Watney's table.

'Is this a tour split?'

'Was this anything to do with the fact that you weren't selected for the first game?'

'Was there anything vindictive in your action?'

Watney grins his way out of danger. 'It is a tour split,' he answers, 'between management and coach. Yes, I saw Ivor Checks squirt the shaving cream all over the manager and then write a dirty note and put it in the manager's top pocket.'

All nine pressmen dash four tables to where the twins, J V Charrington, Checks, Quivermore and Vaux-Tankard are sitting.

'Let's see the note. It's in your top pocket.'

Terry O'Male, one of Fleet Street's most aggressive journalists, is in no mood to be side-tracked. He reaches into the pocket and sure enough there is a note signed by Checks. It's evidence enough for the men from Fleet Street who spend the rest of the lunch break fighting for the only telephone in the restaurant to get copy back to their editors.

Jim Messingham arrives with his 39 supporters just as the restaurant finishes serving lunch. Poor bloody supporters. The tour is almost a week old and they haven't seen a football, never mind a match.

The last two hours of the team's journey is used by the selection committee of Mackeson, McEwan, Quivermore and Vaux-Tankard to name the team for the next match, against Boston All Stars. It's a simple-enough process:

'Just give all the lads who missed the first game a run out and we'll be OK,' says Quivermore. 'All agreed. That's that then. Sort out the room pairings, Stan, and make sure the twins are separated. I promised their mother they could play together but she thought it would be nice for them to share rooms with separate families so more people can see how much better they are than the average person.'

Stan frowns as he looks down the list of names. Then he points at one of the Tetley-Simpkisses. 'OK. Julian, you with . . . let me see . . . Nogger. And Jeremy, you share with Bulmer.'

The bulky West Country hooker is not amused. 'If he so much as farts in my company I'll cripple him.'

Bass stares straight in front, unshaven, then slowly snarls: 'Yer, that's right.'

The room pairings are thrown completely out of order by the number of hosts available when the team get to Boston. Twenty-three tourists and only nine of them. One of their guys is laughing.

'Don't worry 'bout a thing. We'll get you a bed before the week's out. OK, you two centres and you full-back go with Chuck.'

Chuck throws his guests' bags into the back of a pick-up and drives them 26 miles to his house telling them how he likes having them because he plays full-back and centre and was unlucky not to be selected for the USA team that won the 1924 Olympic Final.

The Boston All Stars' prop, Ken Schultz, runs a ranch 55 miles out of town. He is busy telling the lads that they will enjoy the run of his bunkhouse and that if they like they can go to work on the ranch with the other hands at 5.30 tomorrow morning. Schultz is delighted to have all the forwards except Bulmer at his place to meet his wife and eight kids.

'Well, honey,' he says when they arrive. 'This is ten of the meanest critters ever to come out of Britain.'

Ruddle forces a smile and then turns to face the ranch-house which resembles a giant garden shed and smells much the same. Meanwhile the others are being taken by well-meaning families. Eldridge-Pope goes with a stockbroker and his middle-aged wife. One or two of the Boston All Stars turn up to collect someone to look after, then, the break of all breaks: Watney and Younger, who have been left behind, have the choice of a middle-aged rugby heavy who wants to show them Boston and talk about rugby all night, or a pair of lovely 25-year-old divorcees whose only interest is physical and who share a flat close by. The heavy is kind enough to help load the suitcases into the girls' Cadillac and wave as Watney and Younger speed off into suburbia chatting about anything but rugby football.

THE SECOND MATCH

The morning sees the boys training hard, once everyone has managed to find the field. Even Carling is going well now that he's over his tummy upset. J V Charrington is on the field with his arm out of the sling but does not have full movement. The team is announced at the usual press conference and goes as follows:

Usher; Younger, Ansell, O'Guinness, Courage; Eldridge-Pope, Watney; Haig, Bulmer, Bass, Ruddle, Mackeson, Carling, Everard, Theakston. Replacements: Ansell, McEwan.

Injured players: Tetley-Simpkiss, Tetley-Simpkiss, Charrington.

The leading question is asked by Barry Whocombe, one of Fleet Street's more placid people. 'Excuse me, Sir.'

Quivermore looks down like an angry hawk. 'Yes?'

'Why did you choose Eldridge-Pope at outside-half instead of Younger?'

'Eldridge-Pope can play in any position where you can catch it and kick it. You know as well as I do when it comes to running he does leave a little to be desired so we have put Younger there in order to add pace to the flanks.'

Then a stunner from Kri Slander, the son of a Russian diplomat who defected to the West in the Forties; Kri has made his mark in Fleet Street as a straight-talking, hard-writing journalist with the popular *Daily Reflection*:

'Is there any truth in the rumour that the hooker selected for Saturday was limping badly as a result of jumping from a second-floor window of an apartment building after being disturbed by an irate husband as he served the said husband's wife?'

Quivermore begins to sweat and dab his forehead with a dirty grey handkerchief. 'Serve, serve, what do you mean by serve, do you mean serve as in dinner?'

'No, Air Vice-Marshal, I mean serve as in bulls and cows, boars and sows, stallions and mares.'

'Good grief, I must check that out before answering. Let's all meet again in one hour's time. Is that all right?'

Quivermore, Vaux-Tankard and Checks storm off to find Bulmer who's got a card game going with eleven members of the team and a kitty totalling £27. 'Bulmer, come over here at once!'

'But the kitty, sir!'

'At once. And bring Dai Usher with you.'

The Air Vice-Marshal, Checks and Vaux-Tankard start firing questions at the likeable hooker. 'Who was this woman?' 'Is it true?' 'You jumped out of the window?' 'How big was the husband?'

Dai Usher comes over to join the group, and after a brief examination of Bulmer's knee confirms severe bruising but thinks he will be OK to play.

Quivermore considers the situation. 'Right, I'm going into the press conference to tell them it's a training injury and that's all.'

Bulmer stutters: 'You're not going to send me home, then?'

Quivermore doesn't smile, but he doesn't say yes. Later he convinces the Pressgang of the story and so wins the respect of many of the team for sturdily defending one of them. Perhaps he's not such a bad chap after all.

The match itself proves the all-round ability of the team as they run riot with a 32 — 0 victory. Mackeson's over the moon afterwards.

'Just goes to show you what we can do when we get it together.'

Press reports carry stories of the bravery of Dai Usher in defence, of K K and Younger in attack, and how the pack in general murdered them with Bulmer taking five balls against the head thanks to the fine prop play of Topcat and Nogger. 'It was easy,' the modest hooker is quoted as saying. And so to the night's celebration at The Old Bull and Bear.

A QUIET NIGHT OUT

With the official function over quickly, and no Embassy-visiting business to contend with, the boys are out for a quiet spell in The Old Bull and Bear which is in fact a nightclub. Unfortunately the owner of the Bull and Bear is a rugby fanatic and offers the boys free beer all night. Piston cannot believe his ears and is soon into his 13th pint, only three in front of the

TEN STRIPPERS AND THE PIANIST

rest of the team. When a group of ten strippers appear on stage the inevitable happens. Twenty rugby players, all with bruised bodies and having some difficulty in standing, are on-stage under the lights and getting it off along to the music provided for the female artistes. The night is a riot. No-one actually scores though this is more because of the excess of alcohol than the resistance of the ladies concerned. At 3am, with the whole team naked and piles of tour kit on the stage, they sit at the beer-stained tables and contemplate what might have been had they not drunk all that beer.

The kindly club owner offers a good suggestion. 'Shall we go on to GTs then?'

Everyone nods except the twins.

'Where have they gone, the crafty little bastards?' Bass gets to his feet. 'They were here just now.'

No-one can find them so the gin and tonic flows and the whereabouts of the twins becomes a matter of no importance until the morning when, despite monumental hangovers all round, every member of the team wants to know if there is any truth in the rumour now flying about. The story goes that the twins had not drunk their quota of beer. With the bruises sustained in the first match only just visible on their faces, they had taken advantage of the sympathy offered by the ten strippers and dived in where angels fear to tread.

'Apparently Julian had five of them and Jeremy the other five.'

Bass is astonished. 'Please tell me it's all a dream.'

Bulmer is physically sick at the thought as the twins smile their way through the training session, which is unadulterated murder for the rest of the lads. Although the boys still don't like the twins, they have a sneaking respect for their performance last night. 'Five a-piece!' Even McEwan has to shake his head and what's more no-one complains when both Tetley-Simpkisses are chosen for the third match, something which would have been unthinkable at the outset of the tour.

Soon after the morning session the lads set off for Chicago, forgetting that they will be travelling until the next day. Bulmer and Watney do their best to keep the boys alive and happy. After 700 games of cards, 800 games of ludo, 500 games of snakes and ladders, 300 crosswords and countless games of backgammon they are still not there. Finally, after what seems a lifetime, they arrive to be met by more hosts than they require. Great stuff! Everyone looks like getting a bed to themselves. Watney and Younger will never be able to beat their Boston set-up. 'They even cleaned our kit.' Younger shakes his head. 'And their cooking wasn't bad either.'

MEET THE TEAM

Victory is gained in the third match, although it proves slightly harder than expected: a narrow 16–13 affair. The tour is more than halfway through, most of the lads are getting along well, the press are happily phoning their copy away on time, the management handle the PR side of the tour smoothly, and Checks has a full quota of fit players. Yes, an injury-free tour.

There is trouble, however, for our friend the travel agent, for although he got the 39 supporters to the States just after the first match, the bus broke down three miles from the ground for the second match and took them to the wrong place altogether for the third match. Add to that the booking of a hotel that has yet to be built, and the loss of all the baggage en route to it, and you can see that the supporters are not too happy at all. Jim has asked for a meeting with the management of the tour and suggests what can be described as an original idea.

'As these people have come all this way to see you, and with the bad luck we have been having, I wonder could they join in a training session or something, you know, just to say they have played with the players?'

Quivermore is surprised but co-operative. 'Why don't we have a match on the Saturday after the final match? We can play twenty minutes each way. You put fifteen of your supporters in for one half and fifteen for the other.'

'That's great, Air Vice-Marshal. Thanks very much.' Off shoots Messingham to tell his band of supporters the great news. The press get hold of the story and demand to be included in the line-up. Messingham is scratching his head now. He will have to appease the pressmen because they are clients just like the 39 supporters.

O'Male is in no mood to be put off. 'I'm playing scrum-half and I want my eight colleagues on the field with me.'

'OK. Give me some time to sort it out.'

He goes off to select the team from nine journalists and 39 tourists ranging from middle-aged miners from the valleys of Wales, there to spend their life savings, and well-to-do pensioners there to experience their first overseas tour as spectators but perfectly prepared to give it a go on the field of play.

Whilst Messingham deliberates, the players call a kangaroo court.

THE COURT

These courts are now an integral part of every tour and ensure that team discipline is maintained. The penalties dished out to the guilty are usually large amounts of alcohol to be consumed in one gulp. The court officials are democratically elected and Ruddle is to sit during this session as judge while Watney is the prosecuting counsel.

Ruddle has done the job well. He sits on a large round chair which is mounted on the hotel bar with a large black robe to add style and a blonde stage wig for extra effect. Watney reads out the first charge, which is against Bulmer, for bestiality and lowering team standards in that when he jumped into the four-poster bed during the night of lust in the Embassy he knew full well that his partner was the mother of the other three lovelies involved and, moreover, she was so ugly that the lads had nicknamed her Foxhunter after the famous show-jumper.

Watney calls Alan Theakston as the first witness for the prosecution. The rangy No 8 takes no time at all in explaining how he, Bulmer and Ruddle had gone along to watch Everard, O'Guinness, Skolar and Topcat perform with the four young ladies but at no time was the light switched off and it was fairly obvious that the one Bulmer ended up with was very old and her face resembled that of a horse. Watney addresses himself to the witness:

'In your opinion, Mr Theakston, would Bulmer have seen what an ugly old scrubber this woman was before he actually got across her? I beg your pardon my Lord.' Watney nods respectfully towards Ruddle. 'As this is a charge concerning animals, I will rephrase that last sentence. Before he actually mounted her.'

The whole team snigger at Watney's turn of phrase.

'Definitely.' Theakston is loving every minute of it. 'He couldn't possibly miss it when she got her gear off and paraded up and down in front of him.'

'You mean to say he had a chance to inspect her beforehand and yet he still went through with it?'

'Yes, sir.'

Ruddle leans forward, and in his slow London drawl says: 'Bulmer, have you any questions for the witness?'

Before Bulmer can say a word, Ruddle says firmly: 'Thank you, sit down please.'

Watney turns his attention to Bulmer. 'Can you deny any of these things Mr Theakston has just told the court?'

'Yes, I bloody well can. First of all the light was definitely off. Secondly she never paraded up and down in front of me and thirdly she wasn't as bad as he says and what's more he's jealous because he couldn't have her.'

'That's very interesting, Bulmer.'

Watney picks up a point. 'How did you know she wasn't that bad if the light wasn't on and she didn't parade up and down in front of you?'

'Well, all right, I suppose she was pretty bad but I was desperate and I had no chance with any of the young girls. I mean, look at the state of me.'

Ruddle leans back. 'I have heard quite enough. By your own admission, Bulmer, you have mounted this horrible horse without any regard for the standards or feelings of your team-mates. You looked only for your own satisfaction and you must be punished accordingly. You must sink two pints of brown ale straight down without a break while the team watch.'

Eyebrows are raised as Watney reads out the next charge, against Sean O'Guinness and Tony Everard for misuse of a dangerous weapon. Watney begins his address:

'You are both extremely fortunate to have personal dimensions that are the envy of every person who has ever had the privilege of seeing them, but in different ways you have both abused the advantage your Maker gave you. You, O'Guinness, have not only flagrantly ignored your spiritual training, you have by the size of your manhood enticed these attractive young ladies away from your team-mates, thereby severely limiting their sexual opportunities.'

O'Guinness is aghast at the whole tone of the proceedings, and in an attempt to get the thing over as quickly as possible he pleads guilty with nothing to say in mitigation but asks that he is not punished with the drinking of alcohol as this is something he has never done in his life.

'All right.' Ruddle has sympathy. 'I can see you have genuine remorse and I have no intention of forcing you to commit another sin. That would be thoroughly distasteful. I am prepared to give you a complete discharge conditional upon your signing a document agreeing to the transplanting of your now-redundant hampton onto me.'

The lads boo and shout and throw paper cups half full of beer.

'Order! Order!'

Ruddle asks O'Guinness: 'Well?'

'Yes, I'll sign. It's no good to me anyway.'

'Well, then, step down.'

Now it is Everard's turn. His crime is that during the tour he has repeatedly refused to give sexual satisfaction to young ladies who have come to his room pleading for it. On many such occasions he has preferred to watch television, and the good name of the team has been gravely

damaged as a result. After Watney has gathered crushing evidence from several members of the team, Everard faces Judge Ruddle's verdict with trepidation.

'Mr Everard,' pronounces Ruddle, 'you are too smooth for your own good and I find you guilty as charged: misuse of a dangerous weapon. Your punishment has already been arranged. You will spend four consecutive nights in the same bed with the old horse Bulmer was mounting just now.'

The whole room erupts with laughter and clapping and Everard steps down from the dock.

'What's more, if you fail to please that lady we have an even worse sexual task set for you. The Court will recess for one week.'

THE LADIES' COLLEGE

After a comfortable win against Texas Tigers the lads have three wins and a draw under their belts, and the drop-in on Los Angeles for the last five days of the tour is looked forward to with some anticipation. They have done their time in bunkhouses, the homes of middle-aged accountants and professors who thought they were taking in nice English students for a few days, and many are hopeful that they might now get some of the luck Watney and Younger had in Boston, although no member of the team can really complain. They have proved very popular with the female population, that is, with the exception of Checks, Quivermore and Vaux-Tankard. The latter pair are cracking on and it doesn't matter, but Checks is desperate to relieve the tensions of the tour.

The team bus arrives at the Ladies' College almost without being noticed. Then the word spreads that the 'footballers' are here. Women of all shapes and sizes appear from nowhere, even Quivermore raises his eyebrows at the range of talent available. Skolar is on the verge of fainting as one young lady offers to carry his bags to the 23-bed dormitory that has been allocated for the team's use. 'We never get guys in groups like this.' Skolar doesn't say anything but his mind can be heard thinking: 'Aye! And we don't get birds in bundles of 3000 either.'

Off goes the young lady across the courtyard, trying not to appear in difficulty with the bulky suitcase that Skolar has let her carry. Skolar, hands in pockets, walks slightly behind her and a little to her right, searching his brain for something smart or charming to say without appearing to be trying. Then it came in a deep Gwent accent that was both sexual and local:

'Much rape in Los Angeles is there?'

Everyone in the group following Skolar and his new mate stop dead in their tracks.

The girl replies: 'Well, no more than 'Frisco or New York.'

Theakston is first into the dormitory, carrying his own bag with three

66

women in close attendance whose physical make-up ranges from the good to the diabolical. Theakston thanks them for their interest and tells them to piss off.

The other lads arrive, with similarly large escorts. The beds are set out 12 on one side of the room and 12 on the other, rather like a tastefully decorated barrack-room. The realization that they have only been in the room for two minutes and are now sexually outnumbered by 3 to 1 is just too much for some of the lads. The door at the end of the room bangs shut, the latch dropped by a tiny but determined-looking girl judged by Bulmer to be nearer 28 than 21.

'Right, boys,' she says, 'we thought you'd like a real American welcome on your first night in Los Angeles and if you look in the lockers beside your beds you will see a little something.'

Bass nearly pulls the little door off its hinges in his haste to see what goodies are in there.

'Christ, they've given me two bottles of best malt whisky.'

'And me!' comes the cry down the line of beds. Ansell starts to pinch himself.

'Is this a dream? Two bottles of whisky and three birds each.'

Squeals of delight come from the bed nearest the door. The three who have cornered Everard have torn his trousers off and have the shock of their lives. All the ladies in the room rush over for a glimpse. 'Oh, my goodness, will it bite if you stroke it?'

The three girls who claimed Everard, blind as it were, now leave the other girls in no doubt that they alone are to have the opportunity of finding out.

O'Guinness, determined not to get himself into the same situation he found himself in at the Embassy, has his head halfway through the window when he is pulled back by four girls, two on each leg, anxious to see if they have a jackpot like those lucky bitches who chose Everard. The room is alive with the hiss of zips coming down and shoes being pulled off. Each trio of ladies examine their particular men to see if they are all the same as Everard.

Quivermore tries whispering to his bed mate: 'Couldn't we move to somewhere more private?'

The noise from O'Guinness's bed as his manhood is uncovered resembles the Arms Park when Wales score the winner to take the Grand Slam. Two hours later, all the lights are out but still-unsatisfied wenches are prowling the room, lifting blankets for signs of serviceable life.

The whole dormitory sleeps into the morning, when one of the hostesses goes into the kitchen and returns with enough food, alcohol and cigarettes to last for three days. But Topcat Haig is sitting on the edge of the bed, his head in his hands:

'I don't think I can stand three more days of this. We haven't even got a telly to keep us happy during the breaks in the action.'

The days go by and the press and supporters are fooled by rumours that the team has gone off to a special training camp high in the mountains. Meanwhile, Los Angeles Rams announce their team to the waiting pressmen eager to get something off to their editors in London. The Rams manager, Bob Prusmack, surprises everyone by reading the names and profiles of fifteen men who have never played rugby before in their lives, then announces himself as referee, and adds that the Rams have not selected replacements as they do not anticipate any of their men being hurt. The selected team contains four Olympic sprinters and a karate-chop crash-tackler behind the scrum, with five recently demobbed US marines and three convicted murderers currently out on parole up front.

O'Male is furious. 'This is supposed to be a fun tour. Why have you chosen this intimidating combination?'

Prusmack is annoyed at O'Male's attitude. 'I forgot to mention that both half-backs have fought for the world middleweight boxing crown during the last two years.'

Slander has had enough and rushes off to the nearest phone without hearing the rest of the questions. 'Yanks prepare suicide squad! Quivermore's XV prepare at mountain hide-away!' Such is the interest in

REMOTE MOUNTAIN TOP
TRAINING CAMP

the game that the 100,000-seater stadium is sold out before the match, and seats closest to the field of play, and so nearest to the many fatal tackles anticipated, are going at black-market rates.

Match day dawns and the team, at last, surface. One of Messingham's supporters has got wind of the last three-day orgy and spreads the word through the supporters' party. The fact that no mountain camp existed and that three days of bed, birds and booze are no use even to athletes becomes obvious as Quivermore's XV take the field for the last match. Bass throws up on the touch-line, Mackeson and McEwan collapse before they actually reach the field. Referee Prusmack waves a signal to the squad of cheer-leaders on the touch-line and they break into a well-rehearsed song that begins 'Two, four, six, eight . . .' and ends with 'Rams! Rams! Rams!' No member of the team feels any the better when they realize that the cheer-leaders are the same ladies who have been entertaining them for the last three days and who are in fact committed supporters of the Los Angeles Rams.

The game itself is a classic of its kind. The Rams can do everything but catch, the British can do everything but move. Vaux-Tankard, Quivermore and Checks are praying for an honourable draw, and that seems altogether possible as neither team can get within ten yards of the other team's try-line, never mind score. But then comes a break, offering the British their chance to score—and by the only means apparently available to them. Prusmack awards a penalty on the halfway-line, close to touch, after the twelfth karate-chop tackle of the match has felled Tetley-Simpkiss, and almost dissected his windpipe into the bargain. O'Guinness is called up to take the kick but after placing the ball and stepping back towards his touchline his concentration is broken by one of the four young ladies who had abused him in the dormitory. She addresses him Bette Midler-style:

'D'ya wanna nother night like that or are you gonna miss this kick, honey?'

O'Guinness crumples, takes two steps to the right, two steps to the left, falls over the ball and hits it with his left heel. The ball dribbles two yards towards the uprights.

J V Charrington is disgusted. 'Don't let those silly bloody women upset you.' Just then one of those 'silly bloody women' runs onto the field and hits Charrington repeatedly on the head with a brightly coloured umbrella, part of her cheer-leader's uniform. Charrington runs as fast as he has done all tour to the other side of the field and begs K K to swap wings.

Meanwhile the eight meanies selected to play in the Rams pack have begun to get some grasp of Rugby Union. To begin with they had thought every scrum was a huddle, formed *à la* American football to discuss the next tactical move. That suited the British quite well until Nogger gave their hooker a playful nip on the right ear. At the next line-out none of them jumped; instead they each grabbed their opposite number and bit his ear until it bled.

'Wonderful,' Prusmack observed, 'you guys are really learning fast.'

Now Everard is puffing his way across the field and hoping the next ruck will be over by the time he reaches it. 'Don't try any more of those specials will you Nogger?' he pleads.

Checks, jumping up and down on the touchline, is using far more energy than anyone actually playing. 'For Christ's sake let sleeping giants lie. Don't upset them with silly girl's tricks. Play rugby. They'll murder us if it comes to a fight.'

Just then Nogger gets his comeuppance, or return ticket as they say in rugby circles. Their hooker has told Schuman, a six-feet seven-inch black marine playing in the second row, that he would be obliged if he could persuade Nogger not to bite him any more. Schuman's idea of persuasion leaves little doubt that he doesn't want Nogger even to think about biting his hooker again.

The treatment starts with Schuman pulling Nogger's headband down around his throat and then tightening it like an elastic band on a small boy's aeroplane until Nogger turns blue. Then, with play continuing thirty yards away, he pulls Nogger up one-handed by his testicles and asks if he wants any more. Nogger, gasping for air after three minutes of strangulation and three nights of no sleep, is unable to answer. Stubborn, huh? Schuman, still gripping the hapless Nogger by the fruit of his jockstrap, runs at 30 mph to the next ruck, slips on the turf five yards from it and sees Nogger fly right into the ruck and back towards him like a yoyo. 'Still feel stubborn now?' Nogger's voice is strangely high: 'No, no.' Mercifully Schuman decides to let go and get on with the game.

Mackeson has just seen the tactical key to the game and calls his men together while Dai Usher receives treatment for a drooping haemorrhoid that has been troubling him all tour. 'Listen, lads. None of us can run and none of them can catch. Every time we get the ball anywhere in the field drop for a goal in the general direction of the posts. Even if we miss they'll knock it on so we can try more drop goals from the scrums we get.'

The sight of Mackeson, McEwan and Bass dropping for goal sends the whole stadium into hysterics. One American spectator is so amused that he asks an Englishman standing near him: 'Hey! Are these guys as big as Benny Hill back home?'

Funny or not, it works. After 33 attempts, with half a minute to go, Eldridge-Pope, who has come on for the injured or frightened J V Charrington, throws his right leg, drops the ball and, somehow, over it goes. Air Vice-Marshal Ken Quivermore's XV 3 Los Angeles Rams 0.

The boys troop off, heads down but happy at the thought that they have maintained their unbeaten record.

THE GALA DINNER

he end-of-tour dinner is an emotional affair with people encountered in the various places around the USA turning up to say their farewells and to spend their last night together.

The dinner has been arranged by the Los Angeles Rams organizing committee and 250 guests have been invited to this all-male dinner-jacketed piss-up. Quivermore and Vaux-Tankard are arguing about who, apart from the captain, should speak on behalf of the touring team. Vaux-Tankard says that he, as the official RFU representative, should be given the opportunity to speak from that lofty position as well as replying on behalf of the guests as the final speaker of the evening. Quivermore sulks a little but eventually concedes.

The top table is the longest in the room, rather like the backbone of the letter E with three shorter tables extending off it. The fight to sit with the top boys and dignitaries becomes an embarrassment to the organizers because no name places have been set out except a large cardboard sign on the middle table saying 'Players'.

Both teams slurp their way through minestrone soup and jugs of light lagery beer while the disappointed social climbers settle themselves at the side tables. Next on the menu are burger, French fries with side salad and a choice of Thousand Island or blue cheese dressing.

The Rams carve their way through what has become a staple national diet of thousands of Americans. Julian Tetley-Simpkiss complains to Eldridge-Pope who is sitting next to him: 'I say, this transport café food isn't really on, is it?'

Schuman, sitting opposite with the Rams team, leans over with a fork and spears the giant burger on Tetley-Simpkiss's plate. In two mouthfuls it is gone. 'You Limeys sure are fussy.'

Prusmack, in the centre of the top table, accidentally pours ketchup all over the tablecloth as he chats to Quivermore about his ambition to referee a televised international. 'Wouldn't that be just the greatest thing? I mean, me on video!' Quivermore nods politely and then nudges Vaux-Tankard before casting his eyes upward in a 'God forbid!' gesture.

No-one takes too long over the Californian doughnuts with cream and the first speaker is on his feet before coffee is served. The master of ceremonies, Prusmack, has introduced the President of the West Coast Rugby Union to propose a toast to the guests:

'Waal, I would just like to say that it is nice to have you guys over here. You can see that we are still very much novices at the game but we are sure learning fast and you had betta watch out in a couple of years. We are gonna whup your asses!'

American Presidents seem to be no better than ours when it comes to talking non-stop bull-shit without referring to notes, and this one is no exception. After thirty-two minutes, Prusmack is pinching the speaker's leg in a vain attempt to get him back to his chair. On and on he rambles, sending even Nogger Bass to sleep despite the excruciating pain of his badly swollen parts. Finally Prusmack jumps up and says: 'Thank you for that wonderful offering,' and then has to propose the toast to the guests himself as the long-winded President has forgotten his principal task.

'The toast. Our guests.'

Everybody rises and drinks a toast with jugs, glasses, cups or anything they can get their hands on.

Stan Mackeson is next, with the captain's speech. He produces the usual mixture of compliments to them, thank-yous to his own team and modesty in victory. 'You certainly gave us the closest game we have had in the USA and it won't be long before you are taking on and beating established nations at international level.'

Skolar can stand no more of this and aims the remains of a cream-covered doughnut at Stan. It catches him on the side of the head, slides slowly down his face and comes to rest on his shoulder as he struggles to read his speech verbatim from the post card held in his left hand whilst cleaning splashes of cream from the corner of his eye with his right. Generous applause greets the end of Stan's speech as he winds up with a medley of favourite clichés about the game's lasting friendships, and how, though we won the game today, rugby was the real winner, etc, etc.

The Rams' captain, Dave Cusack, has a slightly different style. 'OK you bastards. This is the last losing speech I wanna make this season. From now on we are gonna bite the butt off any team we meet this season. You guys having your first game today will have learned that rugby is not for losers. It just makes the beer taste bad all night. We have been invited along to watch a friendly match tomorrow between Air Vice-Marshal Quivermore's XV and a group of British travelling pressmen and supporters. . . .'

All Quivermore's team for the next day throw their heads back with laughter and pour more beer from the jugs, swapping jokes about killing pressmen and supporters dying of heart attacks before they reach the field. But Cusack is in earnest:

'I would like as many of you as possible to come down and watch the way these guys play the game. We can only benefit from it so let's see as many as possible at the game tomorrow.'

The Rams team had thought Skolar's shot with the doughnut was extremely funny and all part of the British rugby club dinner tradition. On cue from Schuman all fifteen now throw heavy pint pots of beer at Cusack. He is felled. Bulmer rushes forward to the prostrate body and calls for Theakston to administer the kiss of life. Theakston is quick to point out that Jeremy Tetley-Simpkiss has done a course in veterinary science and has passed Part One of the Red Cross Preliminary First Aid Test while still at school. Tetley-Simpkiss arrives, rips off his blazer, takes a look at Cusack and faints into the arms of his brother who starts fanning him with a menu.

Quivermore, red-faced, is panicking. 'For Christ's sake, someone do something.'

Prusmack jumps up and calls a ten-minute piss break before the

final speaker. As Cusack is carried from the hall, O'Guinness and Usher are quietly explaining to the rest of the Rams team that the throwing is normally restricted to buns and custard cakes and that anything like a pint pot is usually considered slightly too heavy. Prusmack, eager to get the show on the road again as quickly as possible, stands and introduces Vaux-Tankard by his full title which really impresses the now-passive Rams:

'Gentlemen, pray silence for the Right Honourable Sir John Vaux-Tankard, Member of the Executive Committee of the Rugby Football Union.'

The Rams' scrum-half, Ed Bruman, is visibly moved. 'Is he related to the Queen at all?'

Watney, trying to do his ambassadorial bit, says: 'Well, not really, but he must have met her when he was knighted.'

'You mean he actually spoke to her?'

Watney smiles at the American's deep interest then settles back in the chair as Vaux-Tankard opens up in comic vein:

'I had intended to start with a tale about Stan Mackeson's sex life but I am told that you are not fond of short stories so I won't go on with that. Of course, you know we became firm friends two years ago when I helped him finish a two-piece jigsaw puzzle.'

The Yanks are cracking up with the wit and delivery of Vaux-Tankard's speech. He continues:

'You may have heard of the personal dimensions of our open-side flanker, Tony Everard. Well, he propositioned a lovely young lady the other night but she warned him that although she was prepared to enjoy sexual relations with him, he ought to know beforehand that she had a bad heart. And Everard, being the gentleman he is, looked her straight in the eye and said: "Well, that's all right, love. You lay on your side and I'll see if I can miss it." Of course, we have one or two crude buggers in our team. Take Nogger Bass for instance. I asked him the other day what was his idea of a woman who was good in bed and after some thought and deliberation, he said slowly: "Well, I think one who lays on her own side and doesn't fart." '

Nogger would have loved to laugh with the others, but he cannot disguise his continuing discomfort. Meanwhile the prestige of Vaux-Tankard is going up by the second. The Rams think he is like this all the time. He comes in with another Tony Everard story:

'He fancied himself so much, you know, that he asked to measure his famous weapon against the longest cat's tail you have ever seen. So Nogger held the cat while Piston measured it against Everard, and do you know after he was declared the loser by three inches he lodged an objection and asked for an official inquiry. And I said to him: "Look, in fairness old chap, you have lost. What's your complaint?" "I want to be measured from the arse, the same as the cat." '

Nearly everyone falls out of his chair at that one; even Nogger manages a broad smile although he doesn't actually move his body. Any movement at all still brings instant pain. Vaux-Tankard winds up with a few thank-yous and presents a President's shield to Prusmack and a Quivermore's XV tie to every member of the Rams team. The drinking goes on into the early hours of the morning. No-one gives much thought to the friendly being played tomorrow.

A FRIENDLY CLIMAX

**S**aturday morning sees Messingham arrive at the training ground with his team of heroes for the twenty-minutes-each-way friendly. O'Male is already changed and directing his Fleet Street legmen into various assorted tracksuit tops and T-shirts.

'Whocombe, you can hook. Slander, prop.'

Terry Hooper, a press agency freelance, has taken off his glasses and wandered away from the group in the hope that O'Male won't see him as he sorts out who will be the other prop. O'Male is incensed at this piece of cowardice.

'Hooper, you prop on the other side.'

Hooper drops his head in shame and walks back to the group who are busy tying bootlaces and rubbing on Vaseline. On the way he treads on and smashes his own spectacles.

'Never mind about that,' says O'Male. 'We'll face you in the right direction.'

O'Male is getting even more agitated as he eyes the group for two decent locks.

'You will have to play lock,' he announces at last, pointing at Tony Bodliments of the *Daily Cornishman*. Bodliments looks bemused and says nothing, just shakes his head and zips up his tracksuit top. However, he can't help but appeal when he hears that Tom Todd of the *Daily Moon* is to partner him.

'Listen, Terry. Neither of us has had any experience of scrummaging, and can't jump to save our lives.'

'Shut up,' snaps O'Male, 'I'm thinking about the back row now. OK, you three play in the back row. Choose your own positions amongst yourselves.'

He points to Colin Epsom, the only photographer in the party, J D Gee of the *Eastern Post* and David Coldman of the *Daily Guardsman*. 'OK, we're ready.'

Messingham is desperate to get something right for a change. 'But Terry, you've got all the pack positions and scrum-half, that only leaves six positions between 39 supporters. Forty if you include me.'

O'Male considers the predicament, one hand on his hip, the other hand under his chin with the index finger over his mouth. 'Come with me, I'll speak to Quivermore.'

Vaux-Tankard and Quivermore are sitting on a park bench with Checks. The light-hearted frolic which is to follow is of little importance as far as they are concerned. O'Male approaches and starts in with the very direct approach for which he is known.

'We have got forty players. It's too many.' He points to Messingham. 'You've got to do the right thing by your supporters and give them all a game.'

'What I'll do,' says Quivermore after a pause, 'I'll put all twenty of my players on the field plus myself and Vaux-Tankard, and you play forty men behind the scrum.'

But the others insist Vaux-Tankard should referee. Quivermore agrees. Half an hour later Vaux-Tankard blows a shrill blast on his whistle. The game is on.

From the first minute O'Male is barking orders to his inadequate pack who, after two scrums and a line-out, are calling for oxygen cylinders to be brought to the touch-line. The game is being played at 200mph with the ball going through hands at an alarming pace, but because of the numbers of bodies on the field of play no-one can break through to the try-line. Things start to go wrong in the fourth scrum of the game and the worst happens. Epsom, J D Gee, Kri Slander and Todd are left writhing in agony as the opposition pack trot away to the next ruck.

O'Male shows no sympathy. 'Get off. You are just cluttering up the field.'

He orders four of the 40 three-quarters on show into the pack and at the same time calls a short penalty move designed to score a vital try before half-time.

'OK, everyone bunch up like a herd of grazing buffaloes and then

charge towards the try-line. I'll slip the ball to the last man in the bunch who will have the path cleared by the rest of you.'

The move is started, and as the herd gathers speed Quivermore's players assemble under the posts grinning at this bizarre ploy. They are nonetheless determined to stop it. The charge is led by the biggest men the supporters can muster: ten large miners from a village just outside Pontypool.

Vaux-Tankard, rather like the helpless witness to a road crash, realizes that the charge is going much too fast as it passes him at around 30mph. He blows hard in a vain bid to stop the collision. Too late. The combined weight of the mob sends hitherto fit bodies flying in all directions. Dai Usher ends up draped over the crossbar. Fourteen others are unrecognizable as they are driven into a large iron grass roller which is behind the dead-ball line. O'Male himself, having passed the ball to the last man, Whocombe, has run into a goal post at full speed while looking across at Whocombe for the return pass. Whocombe in turn has dropped the ball on impact with Bodliments and Coldman, who are stretched out cold. Hooper is walking around, arms outstretched in front of him, trying to figure out what's happened. Quivermore sees the tour in ruins. He stands, ashen-faced, waving his finger at Messingham who somehow seems to be the only man standing after the collision.

'You planned this, didn't you. Well, travel agent or not, let's see you get that bloody lot home.'

The wretched Messingham begins to apply himself to the almost-impossible task of getting 62 cripples home. The ambulances have ferried half the injured off the field by the time he gets his inspiration.

'I know what we want,' he says to himself. 'One of those RAF transport carriers.' He telephones the British Embassy where the staff can still remember the team's visit earlier in the tour.

'Yes, of course we can help you,' comes the answer. 'We'll lend you our biggest transport carrier, wheelchairs, stretchers, and we'll even fit seats for those who are able to sit.'

'Oh, marvellous,' says Messingham.

Just then the news filters through from the British military hospital where all the injured have been taken. Fourteen players, six supporters, and seven members of the press have been certified seriously injured on arrival. Messingham, never one to miss an opportunity, says: 'Can you fix twenty-seven boxes into that carrier as well?'

'Yes, there's plenty of room.'

Messingham is rubbing his hands as the Embassy have agreed to lay on the flight free and he knows he will get a rebate from the airline company on the return flight seats he won't be using.

The flight itself is uneventful apart from the pathetic moaning of the injured, and hours later the entire party is being unloaded at RAF Brize Norton. 'It has been a tour to remember,' wrote Vaux-Tankard that evening in his diary. On a fresh sheet of paper he made the following list while the details were fresh in his memory.

TOUR RECORD

Played	5
Drawn	1
Won	4
Lost	0
Penalties	8
Tries	16
Conversions	3
Points against	17
Deaths	?
Temporarily disabled	6
Permanently disabled	8
Alcoholic poisoning	3
Social diseases	7
Chronically ill	4

AFTERMATH

Both the Tetley-Simpkisses and J V Charrington survived the tour. Jeremy is now parliamentary candidate for Wigan East, and his brother Julian acts as his agent. Charrington has retired from active business and is a sleeping partner in a rubber company. In a letter from the RFU, Air Vice-Marshal Quivermore, Sir John Vaux-Tankard and Able Seaman Ivor Checks have been informed that never again will they be allowed to hold administrative positions within the game of Rugby Union. On his return to London Kri Slander was made editor-in-chief of the *Daily Reflection* and Terry O'Male was offered the chance to fight in a final eliminator for the British welterweight crown. Sean O'Guinness was asked to leave his monastery traineeship after revealing at Confession the goings-on at the British Embassy and in Los Angeles. He now lives alone on a remote hummock off the tip of Iceland.

THE END